BEING SAFE WITH TECHNOLOGY

BY SUSAN KESSELRING • ILLUSTRATED BY DAN McGEEHAN

The Child's World

Published by The Child's World®
1980 Lookout Drive • Mankato, MN 56003-1705
800-599-READ • www.childsworld.com

ACKNOWLEDGMENTS
The Child's World®: Mary Berendes, Publishing Director
The Design Lab: Design and production
Red Line Editorial: Editorial direction

LIBRARY OF CONGRESS CATALOGING-IN-PUBLICATION DATA
Kesselring, Susan.
  Being safe with technology / by Susan Kesselring;
illustrated by Dan McGeehan.
       p. cm.
  Includes bibliographical references and index.
  ISBN 978-1-60954-373-0 (library bound: alk. paper)
  1. Home accidents—Prevention—Juvenile literature. 2. Household
electronics—Safety measures—Juvenile literature. I. McGeehan,
Dan, ill. II. Title.
  TX150.K473 2011
  613.6—dc22   2010040477

Printed in the United States of America
Mankato, MN
December, 2010
PA02069

About the Author
Susan Kesselring loves children, books, nature, and her family. She teaches K-1 students in a progressive charter school down a little country lane in Castle Rock, Minnesota. She is the mother of five daughters and lives in Apple Valley, Minnesota, with her husband, Rob, and a crazy springer spaniel named Lois Lane.

About the Illustrator
Dan McGeehan spent his younger years as an actor, author, playwright, and editor. Now he spends his days drawing, and he is much happier.

Hi! I'm Buzz B. Safe. Watch for me! I'll tell you how to have fun and be safe with technology.

How do you use **technology**? Do you e-mail your best friend on the computer? Are you great at video games?

All this technology helps us learn about the world, keep in touch with each other, and have fun. But it's important to know a few rules that will keep you safe.

Technology is the use of science, skills, and ideas to make new or better things. Machines are made that solve problems or make life easier. A phone is an example of technology. It solves the problem of how to talk to people who are not nearby.

Each family has its own rules about using the phone. When is it okay for you to answer the phone? What should you say when you answer? Just ask your parents.

5

Ring, Ring. "Hello?" You jumped to answer the phone. If the caller is not someone you know, it's best to have an adult talk to him or her. Hand the phone to a parent.

If a caller asks for someone who isn't home, don't let the caller know. Say, "My mom can't come to the phone right now. Who is calling?" Avoid telling a stranger who is or is not at home.

Keep a list of your parents' work numbers and a close friend's or relative's number near the phone. If you ever need to call one of them for help, just check the list.

Video games are another technology that can be lots of fun. Some help you learn. Maybe you've even played a video game in school!

But not all video games are great. Some show things you shouldn't see. Really violent war games are probably not good to play. Talk with your parents about which video games you are allowed to play. Avoid spending all your time gaming, though! Get outside and play with friends, too. Fresh air and active fun keeps you healthy.

You learn a lot from watching television. On a show about Africa, you learn about lions and zebras. Television shows you new things. It is entertaining, too. Some shows make you crack up with laughter!

Check with your parents first, though, before watching. Some television shows are not good for kids. And avoid watching television for too long. You'll miss out on other things—like swinging and playing basketball! Plan out the shows you will watch each week. Then stick to your plan.

Avoid getting stuck in front of the television! Limit what you watch to no more than one or two hours each day.

A computer is like a really big brain—it can store so much information. That makes it a great learning tool. When it's connected to the **Internet**, you can find out almost anything you want to know. A computer also helps you stay in touch with friends. To use it safely, though, you need to know some important rules.

The history of computers dates back hundreds of years. The first computer-like machine was made in the 1600s. Electronic computers began developing in the 1930s and 1940s. The first personal computer came out in 1975. Since then, computers have become much smaller and faster.

When you're **online**, you visit Web sites about almost anything. Try clicking your **mouse** on certain spots on the computer screen. The spots are called **links**. They lead you to other information you want to know— like cool facts about Mars or fun math games.

But clicking on the wrong link can cause problems for your computer. It could also bring you to a Web site that isn't for kids. Always have a parent near you when you are on the Internet. Mom or Dad can tell you if it is safe to click.

On some sites, people can send you messages. You know to be careful around strangers. But on the computer, it is tricky to tell who is a stranger and who is a friend. Some people may pretend to be people they are not. Tell your parents about your online friends. And never plan to meet an online friend without your mom or dad.

There are about 160 billion e-mails sent each day. Junk mail makes up more than 90 percent of these messages.

Just to be safe, some information needs to be kept **private**. Avoid putting your name, picture, age, phone number, and address on the Internet. Also, if you type this information into a public computer, other people might be able to see it. Have your parent check the site out first. And, keep computer **passwords** private, too.

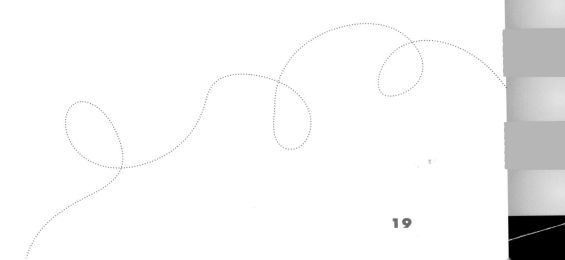

Remember that technology is cool, but it is also just a tool. People, not technology, should be your best friends. Be sure to spend time having fun with friends and family! Use technology wisely and make time for other fun things in your life.

TECHNOLOGY SAFETY RULES TO REMEMBER

Always be safe!

1. Talk with your parents about how and when to answer the phone.

2. Check with your parents about which video games are good for you.

3. With your parents, plan which television shows to watch.

4. Watch no more than one to two hours of television each day.

5. Always have Mom or Dad near you when you are online.

6. Tell your parents about your online friends.

7. Keep your name, age, address, phone number, and passwords private.

8. Remember to spend most of your time with people, not technology.

GLOSSARY

Internet (IN-tur-net): The Internet is the system that allows many computers to connect to each other. You can find a lot of information on the Internet.

links (LINGKS): Links are pictures or words you click on to get to another part of the Internet. Ask your parents if you're not sure if you should click on certain links.

mouse (MOWSS): A mouse is a small oval-shaped tool that you move with your hand to control what happens on your computer screen. Ask your parents before clicking your mouse on a link.

online (on-LYN): Online describes being on the Internet. Ask your parents the rules about going online.

passwords (PASS-wurds): Passwords are secret codes. Sometimes you need passwords to get on your computer or to visit places on the Internet.

private (PRY-vit): If something is private, it is not to be shared with strangers. Keep your computer passwords private.

technology (tek-NOL-uh-jee): Technology is a thing that solves a problem and is made using science. Computers and phones are examples of technology.

TO LEARN MORE

BOOKS

Johnson, Jinny. *Being Safe*. New York: Crabtree Publishing, 2010.

Leavitt, Jacalyn S., and Sally Shill Linford. *Faux Paw's Adventures in the Internet: Keeping Children Safe Online*. Indianapolis, IN: Wiley, 2006.

Sommers, Michael. *The Dangers of Online Predators*. New York: Rosen, 2008.

WEB SITES

Visit our Web site for links about being safe with technology:
childsworld.com/links

Note to Parents, Teachers, and Librarians: We routinely verify our Web links to make sure they are safe and active sites. So encourage your readers to check them out!